For Martin, Ben Played

To Benjamin, my teacher, mentor, and friend.

Deep down in Montgomery there was a special boy.
He loved to play the black and whites, while others played with toys.

He sat at his piano and practiced every day.
The people, they all noticed 'cause oh, how Ben could play!

Ms. Coretta taught Ben music.
Her husband was a preacher man.
Ben just called him **Martin,**
every time he shook his hand.

Ben was never quite as happy

      as when he sat down at those keys.

With Ms. Coretta guiding him,

             he **painted melodies.**

Martin planned to **change the world!**

His work brought lots of fame;

he fought to make things better, and people learned his name.

Ben loved music and loved languages.
He was **brave** and he was **bold.**

He went to college in Atlanta
    when he was just sixteen years old!

Ben always tried his hardest, and he got perfect grades.
For every question, he found an answer,
and he loved to use his brain.

But Ben best showed his talents when he sat down at those keys.

When he **shared his gift of music,**

things got quiet, the world would freeze.

And yes, he loved the classics;
he loved Strauss and he loved Bach.

But when he sat down at an organ,

he could make the **whole room rock!**

When his classes ended, Ben would find a place to play,
but he skipped a day of practicing when he got a call one day.

Ben was sitting on his bed
 when the phone call came.

Martin was gone too soon;
 life would never be the same.

Ben put his face in his hands and felt tears in his eyes.
He knew he would miss his friend.

He wished he'd said goodbye.

Ben didn't waste a minute. He went to be with family.
No one knew that he was coming,
    but it was where he had to be.
The world was wrapped in sadness, many dressed in black,

but **all the love,**

from **all the people,**

couldn't bring Martin back.

Ben smiled when he saw Coretta.

        She looked sad, and she looked nervous.

The people all seemed restless
      as they planned the funeral service.

The organist was sick from sadness.
What was wrong? No one could say.
        It was clear he couldn't do his job.

Coretta said,

"Ben, **you'll have to play.**"

With little time to ready,

Ben practiced in the empty room.

The church was dark and quiet, but it would be full real soon!

People thought Ben might get frightened,

but there was no time for fear.

Ben would play for Martin so all the world could hear!

The room filled up with people.

Music came from Ben's fingertips.

The world came to honor Martin,

and Ben watched their teardrops drip.

There was **power** in the moment, but no words to say.

A young man, a fallen friend—

for Martin, Ben played.

Taking Action

Ben lived a life of service. We will honor his legacy by giving a percentage of the proceeds to each of the following organizations:

- **The Memorial to Peace and Justice** in Ben's childhood home of Montgomery, Alabama.

- **The Ben Ward Arts Endowment at Duke University**, where Ben's legacy is honored by giving students the ability to experience the arts.

- **Reach Incorporated**, a nonprofit literacy organization in Washington, D.C. founded by this book's author.

Sell your books at sellbackyourBook.com!
Go to sellbackyourBook.com
and get an instant price quote.
We even pay the shipping - see
what your old books are worth
today!

00020624303

062 **4303**   **G**

Mark Hecker

Mark is an educator, currently living and working in Washington, D.C. As a student at Duke University, he was a singer in The Pitchforks of Duke University. Ben, the subject of this book, was a Tenor II and the group's faculty advisor. Since Duke, Mark has dedicated his life to helping teens become successful students and community leaders. He is currently the executive director of Reach Incorporated, a nonprofit organization in the District of Columbia.

You can contact him at mark@reachincorporated.org.

Song Nguyen

Born and raised in Vermont, Song has always been inspired by the colors of the natural environment. Though art was her favorite class in high school, she focused on other things during her time at the University of Vermont. A self-taught artist, Song believes strongly in using art as a tool to engage communities. Through art and her career in public health, she hopes to continue supporting under-resourced communities, both domestically and abroad. This is Song's first children's book.

You can see more of her work at www.songnguyenart.com.

Benjamin Ward

Raised in Montgomery, Alabama, Ben was a musical prodigy who took piano lessons from Coretta Scott King and went on to play the organ at Dr. King's 1968 memorial service in Atlanta. Ben was a graduate of Morehouse College and Yale University. Starting in 1980, Ben served as a dean and professor of Philosophy, Arabic, and Germanic Studies at Duke University. He remained at Duke until his death in 2013.

During his battle with Cancer, Ben kindly shared stories of his childhood with this book's author. This story is based on those conversations.

Acknowledgements

This story came to life over many years as I witnessed Ben's illness and eventual death. His story was one that I felt had to be shared. But, I knew that I could not do this alone. I am so appreciative to all those who played a role in making this book a reality. Many friends read early drafts and suggested valuable edits. I was energized by the excitement several early readers shared.

The words came to life on the page thanks to Song's incredible illustrations. I am so thankful that I lucked into meeting her through her work in public schools. Once the words and the illustrations were complete, Kelly used her exceptional design skills to bring them together to create a beautiful book. Thank you both for lending your time and your efforts to a project so meaningful to me.

I'm also thankful to my mother, my brothers, and the rest of my family for providing encouragement along the way. I have gratitude for my father, whose loss continually inspires me to capture stories too important to lose. And, finally, I can't imagine doing this without Elizabeth, my love, whose support and pride mean so much.

Mark Hecker
June 2017

CPSIA information can be obtained
at www.ICGtesting.com
Printed in the USA
BVOW05s0730300917
496372BV00021B/478/P